GREATEST TEAMS THAT DIDN'T WIN IT ALL

BY WILL GRAVES

CAMILLUS

THE WILD WORLD OF SPORTS

SportsZone

An Imprint of Abdo Publishing
abdopublishing.com

abdopublishing.com

Published by Abdo Publishing, a division of ABDO, PO Box 398166, Minneapolis, Minnesota 55439.

Printed in the United States of America, North Mankato, Minnesota
102017
012018

THIS BOOK CONTAINS
RECYCLED MATERIALS

Cover Photos: Paul Sancya/AP Images, foreground; Mark J. Terrill/AP Images, background
Interior Photos: Winslow Townson/AP Images, 4–5; Henny Ray Abrams/AP Images, 6; Elaine Thompson/
AP Images, 7; Paul Spinelli/AP Images, 9; NFL Photos/AP Images, 10; Vernon Biever/AP Images, 12; AP
Images, 13, 19, 41, 42, 43; Al Messerschmidt/AP Images, 15; Peter Southwick/AP Images, 16; Alex Brandon/
AP Images, 20, 33; Jeff Chiu/AP Images, 22; Eric Risberg/AP Images, 23; Kevork Djansezian/AP Images,
25, 27; Ric Francis/AP Images, 26; Lennox McLendon/AP Images, 28; John Swart/AP Images, 31; Gene J.
Puskar/AP Images, 32; Al Behrman/AP Images, 34; Larry Reese/Houston Chronicle/AP Images, 36–37; LM
Otero/AP Images, 38; Bill Nichols/AP Images, 44

Editor: Patrick Donnelly
Series Designer: Craig Hinton

Publisher's Cataloging-in-Publication Data

Names: Graves, Will, author.
Title: Greatest teams that didn't win it all / by Will Graves.
Description: Minneapolis, Minnesota : Abdo Publishing, 2018. | Series: The wild world of sports | Includes
     online resources and index.
Identifiers: LCCN 2017946931 | ISBN 9781532113642 (lib.bdg.) | ISBN 9781532152528 (ebook)
Subjects: LCSH: Sports--United States--History--Juvenile literature. | Sports--Miscellanea--Juvenile
     literature.
Classification: DDC 796--dc23
LC record available at https://lccn.loc.gov/2017946931

TABLE OF
CONTENTS

ALMOST PERFECT

Some teams seem to have it all: star players, savvy coaches, talent at every position. They're heavy favorites to finish the season with a trophy in hand and a victory parade on the way.

But sometimes that big celebration day never arrives. Sometimes another team stands in the way, puts it all together, and pulls off a massive upset. And the "greatest team" goes home empty-handed.

That's what happened to the 2007 New England Patriots. From 2001 to 2004 the Patriots had won three Super Bowls behind quarterback Tom Brady and head coach Bill Belichick. After coming up short the next two seasons, the Patriots were ready to make another run in 2007. They signed star wide receiver Randy Moss and took aim at perfection.

New England embraced the challenge. The Patriots set a flurry of National Football League (NFL) records. They scored 589 points,

Wide receiver Randy Moss shattered records in his first season with the Patriots.

an average of more than 36 points per game. Brady tossed a record 50 touchdown passes. Moss hauled in 23 of them. All of those were records. The Patriots finished the regular season 16–0 and won two playoff games to reach the Super Bowl. But the National Football Conference (NFC) champion New York Giants got the last laugh.

The Giants had lost to New England in the last game of the regular season and barely made the playoffs. But quarterback Eli Manning got hot and led the team to three straight wins on the road in the postseason. That put the Giants in New England's path to perfection, and they weren't about to get steamrolled.

New York kept Brady in check for most of the game. But finally, with less than three minutes to play, Brady found Moss for a touchdown pass. That gave the Patriots a 14–10 lead. Perfection was in reach. But it was not to be. Down to one last

Tom Brady and the Patriots beat the Giants to finish the season 16–0. But the playoffs would be a different story.

Tyree, *left*, holds off Harrison to make the big catch.

chance, Manning escaped a pass rush near midfield and heaved the ball toward backup wide receiver David Tyree, who was one-on-one with Patriots safety Rodney Harrison at New England's 25-yard line.

Tyree jumped and pinned the ball to his helmet. It was one of the most amazing catches in football history. The Patriots were stunned. The Giants took the lead four plays later, and New England's shot at 19–0 was gone. Although the Patriots have won more championships since, the one that got away still stings.

SUPER BOWL STUNNER

n 1994 Kurt Warner was bagging groceries at a store in Iowa. He made $5.50 an hour and hoped his football career wasn't over.

Seven years later, Warner was a two-time winner of the NFL's Most Valuable Player (MVP) Award. The quarterback with the lightning-quick release led an offense that had one of the coolest nicknames ever: the Greatest Show on Turf.

The St. Louis Rams won the Super Bowl after the 1999 season with Warner, star running back Marshall Faulk, and wide receivers Isaac Bruce and Torry Holt lighting up the scoreboard.

In 2001 the Rams were even better, going 14–2 during the regular season. Faulk scored 21 touchdowns. Bruce and Holt both topped 1,100 yards receiving. They appeared to be unstoppable.

But the New England Patriots found the recipe to stun St. Louis in the Super Bowl. Adam Vinatieri kicked a last-second field goal to give New England the 20–17 win. And just like that, the curtain came down on the Greatest Show on Turf.

Adam Vinatieri connects on a 48-yard field goal to end the Rams' dreams of winning another Super Bowl.

NFL NIGHTMARE

The 1968 Baltimore Colts entered the season with high hopes. Then star quarterback Johnny Unitas hurt his right arm in a preseason game.

Backup Earl Morrall was capable, and the way the Colts played defense in 1968, that's all he needed to be. Baltimore allowed only 10 points a game, the best in the NFL. Linebacker Mike Curtis and cornerback Bobby Boyd were first-team All-Pro selections for a defense that put a vice grip on the league. In a six-game stretch late in the season, the Colts allowed just one touchdown and 22 total points.

Baltimore went 13–1 to easily win its division. Morrall led the league with 26 touchdown passes. He played so well that he kept the starting job even when Unitas healed from his injury.

Earl Morrall filled some big shoes for the Colts in 1968.

The Jets didn't give Baltimore running back Tom Matte much room to run.

The Colts stormed into the Super Bowl after crushing Minnesota and Cleveland in the NFL playoffs. The New York Jets and star quarterback Joe Namath were waiting in Miami. The Jets were the champions of the rival American Football League (AFL).

MORRALL AUTHORITY

Morrall and the Colts made up for the loss two years later. The Colts reached Super Bowl V against the Dallas Cowboys. Unitas left with an injury, and Morrall came on to help Baltimore win 16–13. Morrall earned another Super Bowl ring two years later with the Miami Dolphins. He led the team to nine wins while starter Bob Griese healed from a broken ankle.

Many people thought the teams in the AFL could not match up with the NFL powers. The Green Bay Packers easily won the first two Super Bowls against the AFL champions. Super Bowl III between the Colts and Jets was supposed to be more of the same. Experts picked the Colts to win by more than two touchdowns.

Namath didn't agree. He said before the game that the Jets would win. It was a bold statement, but he and the Jets backed it up. Baltimore's defense came to play, but Morrall threw three interceptions and the offense couldn't get much going. Not even a late appearance by Unitas could prevent a 16–7 upset by the upstart Jets.

Joe Namath did just enough to back up his pregame talk as the Jets scored a huge win for the AFL.

WIDE LEFT

The Minnesota Vikings had a high-powered offense in 1998. Rookie Randy Moss caught 17 touchdown passes. Quarterback Randall Cunningham revived his career with an amazing season. Wide receiver Cris Carter and running back Robert Smith made the Pro Bowl. The Vikings scored a then-NFL record 556 points and lost just once all season as they rolled to the NFC championship game.

The Atlanta Falcons were no slouch at 14–2. But playing on the road in Minnesota, they trailed by a touchdown with just over two minutes to go. It looked bleak for the Falcons when Minnesota kicker Gary Anderson came on to extend his team's lead to 10 points. Anderson had not missed a kick all season, going 39 for 39. One more field goal and Minnesota was likely Super Bowl–bound.

Instead, the 38-yard kick sailed wide left. The Falcons took advantage of the break. They rallied to tie the score against the shocked Vikings. Then they won it in overtime, leaving the Vikings to wonder how they could have let that opportunity slip away.

Cris Carter and the Vikings had a season to remember in 1998, but they came up one game short of the Super Bowl.

BROTHERS BASHED

The Oakland Athletics had two of baseball's biggest sluggers in the late 1980s. Mark McGwire and Jose Canseco called themselves the "Bash Brothers." Every time one of them hit a home run, they celebrated by slamming their forearms together. They combined for 74 home runs in 1988. Closer Dennis Eckersley led the major leagues with 45 saves. The A's won 104 games and made it to the World Series for the first time in 14 years.

The Los Angeles Dodgers awaited the A's. In Game 1 Oakland took a 4–3 lead into the bottom of the ninth thanks to a grand slam by Canseco. Eckersley came on to finish off the Dodgers. After two quick outs, Eckersley walked a batter. Los Angeles sent out star slugger Kirk Gibson as a pinch hitter. Gibson couldn't run because of a leg injury. That didn't stop him from hitting a two-run homer to give the Dodgers a stunning win.

Los Angeles went on to win the series in five games. The Bash Brothers would have to wait another year to win the World Series.

Mark McGwire, *left*, and Jose Canseco battered opposing pitchers in 1988.

CHAPTER 6

WALK-OFF SHOCK

No Major League Baseball (MLB) team has won more World Series than the New York Yankees. But one of their few October failures ranks among the most famous moments in baseball history.

The 1960 Yankees featured sluggers Mickey Mantle and Roger Maris at the top of their game. Mantle hit 40 home runs that season. Maris clubbed 39. The Yankees won the American League pennant, but they were undone by a slick-fielding second baseman for the Pittsburgh Pirates named Bill Mazeroski.

The World Series came down to Game 7 at Forbes Field in Pittsburgh. After 8 1/2 seesaw innings, Mazeroski led off the bottom of the ninth in a tie game. He wasn't much of a power hitter, having hit just 11 home runs that season. But he slammed the second pitch he saw over the wall in left-center field to give the Pirates a 10–9 victory and a surprise World Series championship.

Fans rush the field as Bill Mazeroski rounds the bases after his World Series–winning home run.

MEMORIES OF MAZ

Pirates fans still celebrate Mazeroski's big hit. Every year on October 13, the anniversary of Game 7, fans gather near the spot where Mazeroski's ball cleared the Forbes Field wall to listen to a radio broadcast of the game. It is still the only time a team has won the World Series on a walk-off homer in Game 7.

WILTING WARRIORS

For a long time the key to having a great National Basketball Association (NBA) team was simple. You needed a big man like Bill Russell or Shaquille O'Neal. If you didn't have a big guy, you needed to have an unstoppable star such as Michael Jordan or LeBron James. A wise veteran coach on the bench like Red Auerbach or Phil Jackson helped, too.

The Golden State Warriors didn't have any of those things. Guard Stephen Curry was supposed to be too small to make it in the league. Forward Draymond Green was supposed to be too short to defend other teams' big men. Steve Kerr didn't have any coaching experience when he took over the team in 2014.

All the Warriors did in Kerr's first season was turn the league on its head. Curry and guard Klay Thompson earned the nickname "Splash Brothers" for the way their three-pointers would fly through the net. Green became one of the best defenders in basketball. He could shut

Stephen Curry became a two-time NBA MVP in 2015–16.

down guards, forwards, and centers alike. The Warriors won their first league title in 40 years when they beat the Cleveland Cavaliers in the NBA Finals in 2015.

With everybody back for another run the next season, a second title seemed like a sure bet. Golden State won its first 24 games, something no team had ever done. The Warriors did it even with Kerr missing half the season to recover from back surgery.

Golden State kept winning and winning and winning. The Warriors finished the regular season 73–9, the best record in NBA history. Curry broke his own record for most three-pointers made in a season and won his second straight NBA MVP Award. Then the team breezed through the playoffs before taking a 3–1 lead in a finals rematch with Cleveland.

Then it all fell apart. Green was suspended one game for kicking one of the Cavaliers. Without him,

Klay Thompson, *left*, and Draymond Green played huge roles in the Warriors' success.

In the end, LeBron James and the Cavaliers were too much for the Warriors to handle.

the Warriors lost Game 5. The series headed back to Cleveland, where the Cavs took Game 6, too.

Then in Game 7, back on their home court, the Splash Brothers became the Crash Brothers. Thompson and Curry combined to make just 6 of 24 three-point attempts. James carried Cleveland down the stretch as the Cavs pulled it out 93–89 to win their first NBA championship. After winning 73 games in the regular season, the Warriors fell one victory shy of their second straight title.

LOS ANGELES FAKERS

The Los Angeles Lakers had two of the NBA's biggest stars in the early 2000s. Center Shaquille O'Neal and guard Kobe Bryant teamed with coach Phil Jackson to win three straight NBA titles from 2000 to 2002.

Los Angeles fell short in 2003. So O'Neal called a couple of friends to help out. Forward Karl Malone had played for the Utah Jazz for 18 seasons. The Jazz reached the finals in 1997 and 1998, only to lose to Michael Jordan and the Chicago Bulls both times. Similarly, Gary Payton had been a nine-time All-Star guard while playing for the Seattle SuperSonics since 1990. Payton and the Sonics reached the finals in 1996. They also lost to Jordan and the Bulls, who happened to be coached by Jackson.

With their careers winding down, Malone and Payton wanted badly to earn a championship ring, so they decided to join forces with O'Neal and Bryant. The called themselves "the Big Four."

Kobe Bryant, *right*, led the Lakers to the NBA Finals in 2004.

It took time for the four stars to learn to play together. But by the time the playoffs began, the Lakers were rolling. O'Neal was the big man in the middle. Malone, nicknamed "the Mailman" because he always delivered, knocked down jump shots and grabbed rebounds. Bryant slashed to the hoop for dunks. Payton ran the show as the point guard, getting the ball to his teammates.

The Lakers roared through the Western Conference playoffs. They were heavy favorites to take care of the Detroit Pistons in the finals. But somebody forgot to tell the Pistons they had no chance. Though the Detroit roster wasn't filled with future Hall of Famers, its defense frustrated the Lakers. The series turned in Game 3, when Los Angeles scored just 68 points in a blowout loss as Detroit took a 2–1 series lead. The Lakers averaged just 81.8 points per game in the finals. That's 17 points fewer than they scored during the regular season.

The Pistons won in five games, and the Big Four was no more.

Gary Payton, *left*, and Karl Malone joined the Lakers in 2003 in search of a championship ring.

CHAPTER 9

SHARK BAIT

Detroit Red Wings fans have a tradition during home playoff games. At some point a fan will throw an octopus onto the ice. Fans believe it will give the team good luck. The 1993–94 Red Wings should have been on the lookout for sharks instead.

Detroit was led by center Sergei Fedorov. The Russian star amassed 120 points and won the Hart Trophy, given to the MVP of the National Hockey League (NHL). The Red Wings led the league in goals and entered the postseason as the top seed in the Western Conference. They were heavy favorites to steamroll their way to the Stanley Cup Final.

Their first-round opponents, the San Jose Sharks, finished the regular season with a losing record. They were the last team to qualify for the playoffs. The Red Wings were supposed to make quick work of the Sharks. Instead, the Sharks made history. San Jose stunned Detroit to win the series in seven games. For once, the octopuses in Detroit were safe.

Sharks goalie Arturs Irbe makes a big save in San Jose's Game 7 upset of the Detroit Red Wings in 1994.

OH NO, MARIO!

The Pittsburgh Penguins were the two-time defending Stanley Cup champions going into the 1992–93 season. The Penguins had two of the greatest players in NHL history on their roster in forwards Mario Lemieux and Jaromir Jagr.

The quest for a third straight Cup was not easy. Lemieux wasn't feeling well in January. His doctors told the superstar he had a form of cancer. Lemieux missed two months. He spent most of his time resting and taking medicine to help manage his disease.

When Lemieux returned in March, his team was in a bit of trouble. Pittsburgh trailed Montreal in the race for the league's best record. But with No. 66 back in the lineup, the Penguins hit the gas. Pittsburgh won a record 17 straight games near the end of the regular season. Lemieux punctuated the streak with a five-goal outburst in a 10–4 win over the New York Islanders on April 9.

Mario Lemieux skates with the Stanley Cup in 1992 after the Penguins won their second straight NHL championship.

Jaromir Jagr, *right*, was a dynamic young forward for the great Penguins teams of the early 1990s.

"Super Mario" led the NHL in scoring with 160 points (69 goals, 91 assists) even though he missed 24 games while undergoing treatment. The Penguins earned the Presidents' Trophy for finishing with the best record in the NHL. A third straight Stanley Cup seemed like a sure thing.

The Penguins stormed past the New Jersey Devils in the first round. The New York Islanders were up next. The Islanders were missing their leading scorer, center Pierre Turgeon, because of an injury. They looked like easy pickings.

Lemieux can't seem to believe it as the Islanders celebrate a third-period goal in Game 6 of the conference finals.

The Islanders took Game 1 to send a message they would not go quietly. The Penguins responded and took a 3–2 lead in the series when Lemieux scored two goals in a 6–3 victory in Game 5.

One more win would send Pittsburgh to the conference finals. But the march of the Penguins stopped there. The Islanders took Game 6 at home to force a deciding Game 7 in Pittsburgh. The game went into overtime, and New York's David Volek, who had scored just eight goals all season, netted the winner that shocked the hockey world.

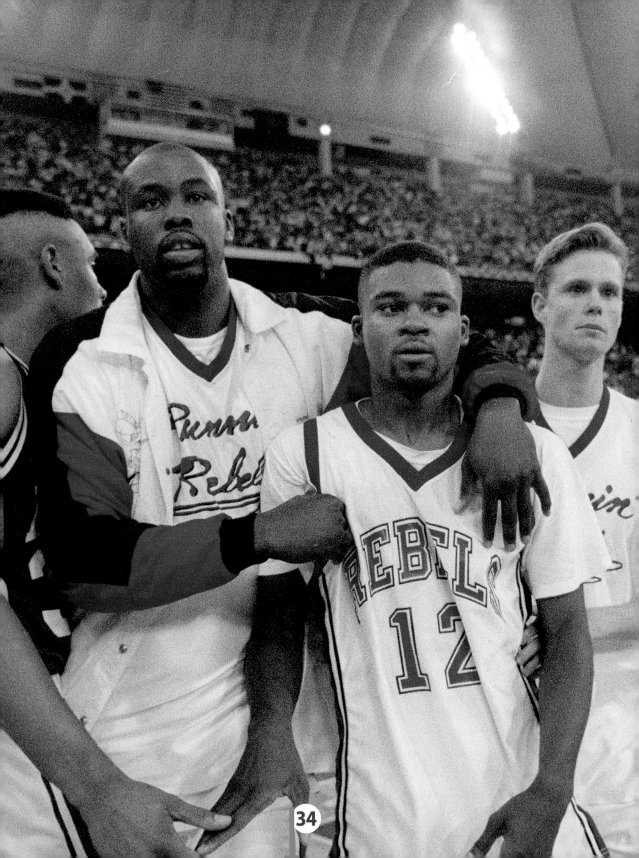

REBELS RUINED

In 1990 the men's basketball team at the University of Nevada, Las Vegas (UNLV) showed why people often referred to them as the "Runnin' Rebels." UNLV raced to the national title, crushing Duke by 30 points in the championship game.

The next season, behind All-American forwards Larry Johnson and Stacey Augmon and coach Jerry Tarkanian, UNLV was even better. The Runnin' Rebels won their first 34 games to reach the Final Four. All but two of those games were decided by 10 points or more. UNLV needed two more victories to become the first team to go unbeaten since Indiana in 1976.

Duke was back for a rematch in the national semifinals. The Blue Devils were ready. UNLV led by just two points at halftime. In a rare close game, the Runnin' Rebels stumbled late. Duke's Christian Laettner hit two free throws to give Duke the lead with 12 seconds left. UNLV had one more chance. However, Anderson Hunt's long three-pointer at the buzzer was off the mark, and UNLV's dream season ended in a nightmare.

A dejected Anderson Hunt (12) and his UNLV teammates leave the court after Duke's Final Four upset in 1991.

CHAPTER 12

COUGARS COME UP SHORT

Lots of college students join fraternities and sororities. In the early 1980s the University of Houston basketball team started a "fraternity" of sorts. It was called "Phi Slama Jama," as in "slam dunk," something the Cougars did a lot.

There wasn't a rim in college basketball that Houston and its team of skywalkers didn't rattle. Behind Akeem "the Dream" Olajuwon and Clyde "the Glide" Drexler, the Cougars dunked their way into the national championship game. Houston threw down 13 slams in a Final Four victory over Louisville. Only North Carolina State stood in the way of a title.

The Wolfpack played tough defense to keep Olajuwon, Houston's star center, in check. Drexler spent much of the game on the bench in foul trouble. The Cougars opened a small lead, but they missed free throws down the stretch that could have clinched the victory.

That was all the opening the Wolfpack needed. With the score tied 52–52 and time running out, guard Dereck Whittenburg launched a long shot. It missed everything. But Wolfpack forward

Houston's Renaldo Thomas can't believe his Cougars lost to North Carolina State.

Lorenzo Charles rose up out of nowhere and dunked the air ball just before the buzzer. Houston was stunned. The men of Phi Slama Jama had picked a bad time to stay grounded.

BULLDOGS BITE

In all college sports, players graduate and move on, so a team's performance varies year to year. But the University of Connecticut (UConn) women's basketball team has been consistently successful. UConn won its first national title in 1995. Two decades later the school had become a championship factory. When they cut down the nets after the 2016 title game, it marked the Huskies' fourth straight title and 11th in 22 years.

Another crown seemed to be on the way in 2017. The Huskies rolled into the national Final Four on a 111-game winning streak. That's the most ever by any major college basketball team. They met Mississippi State University in the semifinals. A year earlier, UConn beat the Bulldogs by 60 points. The loss stuck with Mississippi State. The team put the number "60" in the weight room to remind the players of the defeat. Revenge proved sweet. Mississippi State guard Morgan William hit a shot at the buzzer to pull off a 66–64 upset, one of the biggest in women's basketball history.

Blair Schaefer (1) and Morgan William (2) celebrate after William's buzzer-beater snapped UConn's 111-game winning streak.

RED ARMY REGRETS

In the 1970s the Soviet Union hockey team was often referred to as "the Red Army." That's because the players really were in the army. Only their job was not to fight in wars, but to play hockey. They frequently traveled the world to showcase their firepower.

The core of the team was the so-called "Green Unit." It was led by defensemen Slava Fetisov and Alexei Kasatonov and right wing Sergei Makarov. Vladislav Tretiak, widely considered the best goalie in the world, was a brick wall in the net.

At the time, Soviet players were not allowed to play in the NHL. The Red Army instead chose to demonstrate their greatness at major international tournaments. The Soviets rolled to the gold medal at the 1964, 1968, 1972, and 1976 Winter Games. During the 1976 Olympics, the Soviet team scored 40 goals and allowed only 11.

It figured to be more of the same at the 1980 Winter Olympics in Lake Placid, New York. The Soviets spent the weeks before the Olympics playing in exhibition games in North America. One of them was a 10–3 victory over the US team, a collection of college kids playing under University of Minnesota coach Herb Brooks.

Team USA surprised the Soviets with their effort in the medal round at the 1980 Winter Olympics.

The teams met again in the Olympics. The Soviets came into the game on a roll. They had beaten Japan 16–0 and the Netherlands 17–4. Team USA and its ragtag group of college players were supposed to be no match for the mighty Red Army.

But the home crowd, many of them waving American flags, gave the US team a boost. The Americans scored a goal late in the first period to tie the score. The Soviets pulled Tretiak and replaced him with backup Vladimir Myshkin.

Alexei Kasatonov (7), coach Viktor Tikhonov, and
Slava Fetisov watch helplessly as time runs out in the Soviets'
stunning loss to Team USA.

The plan backfired. The Americans took a 4–3 lead when Mike Eruzione beat Myshkin midway through the third period. The Red Army pressed for the equalizer, but the Americans held on to win.

Team USA clinched the gold medal two days later when it defeated Finland. The Soviets had to settle for the silver medal, but they got to bear witness to "the Miracle on Ice."

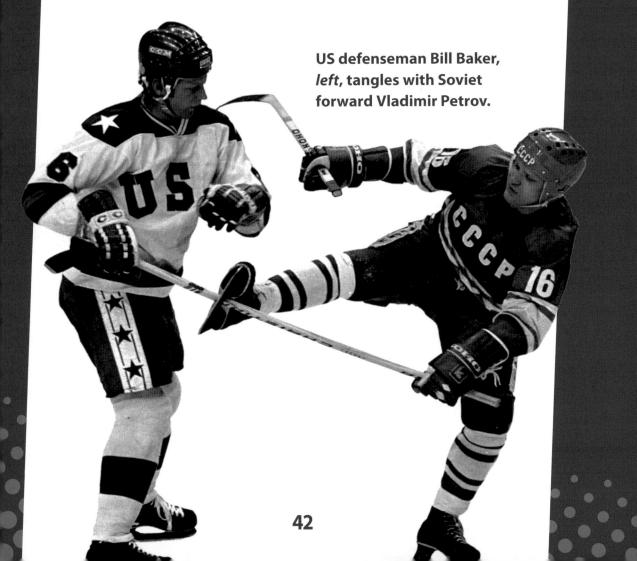

US defenseman Bill Baker, *left*, tangles with Soviet forward Vladimir Petrov.

TROJANS TOPPLED

The University of Southern California (USC) is in Los Angeles. Its 2005 football team was a good fit with the star-laden city. The Trojans entered the season as the defending national champions. They won with style, thanks to cool quarterback Matt Leinart and dynamic running back Reggie Bush.

The Trojans went undefeated during the regular season to extend their winning streak to 34 games. They faced a strong team from the University of Texas in the national title game at the Rose Bowl.

USC's shot at back-to-back championships ended in one of the greatest games in college football history. Leinart passed for 365 yards and a touchdown, and Bush had 177 yards of total offense as USC built a 38–26 lead midway through the fourth quarter.

The Trojans tried to seal the win by going for it on fourth down late in the game. When they didn't make it, Texas quarterback Vince Young took over. Young ran for 200 yards and three touchdowns that day. The last came with 19 seconds to play. Texas won 41–38 as USC's streak came crashing to a halt.

Reggie Bush tumbles into the Rose Bowl end zone, but Texas would get the last laugh in the 2005 national championship game.

GLOSSARY

air ball
A shot that completely misses the basket.

closer
A pitcher who comes in at the end of the game to secure a win for his team.

dynamic
Energetic or forceful.

exhibition
A game that doesn't count in the standings.

fraternity
A student organization for men at a college or university.

gold medal
The award given to the winners of an Olympic event.

pinch hitter
A player who bats in place of a teammate.

point guard
The player who directs a team's offensive attack.

semifinals
The second-to-last round of play in a tournament; the winner of a semifinal game advances to the championship game.

sorority
A student organization for women at a college or university.

upset
An unexpected victory by a supposedly weaker team or player.

ONLINE RESOURCES

To learn more about legendary teams that fell short, visit **abdobooklinks.com**. These links are routinely monitored and updated to provide the most current information available.

MORE INFORMATION

BOOKS

Berman, Len. *The Greatest Moments in Sports: Upsets and Underdogs*. Naperville, IL: Sourcebooks Jabberwocky, 2012.

Graves, Will. *NFL's Top 10 Upsets*. Minneapolis, MN: Abdo Publishing, 2017.

Wilner, Barry. *Biggest Upsets of All Time*. Minneapolis, MN: Abdo Publishing, 2016.

INDEX

ABOUT THE AUTHOR

Will Graves has spent more than two decades as a sportswriter for several newspapers and the Associated Press, covering MLB, the NFL, the NHL, and the Olympics. He also has authored more than a dozen children's sports books. He lives in Pittsburgh, Pennsylvania, with his wife and their children. He still can't believe the Warriors blew that lead against the Cavs.